So, why a cookbook about using things that go “Oink”

Well, I’ll just tell you why. Those porkers may be kinda silly looking critters, but they carry around some of the best eats in the western two thirds of the universe.

And, this cookbook tells you some of the best recipes alive for turning those curly-tailed wonders into some really nummy stuff.

COOKIN' WITH THINGS THAT GO "OINK"

Hearts 'N Tummies Cookbook Co.

1854 - 345th Ave.

Wever, IA 52658

800-571-2665

GENERAL INDEX

SOUPS

Soups & Chowders

HOMEMADE BEAN SOUP

1 lb. dried beans
Water
1 meaty ham hock or pork bones
½ C. chopped onion
2 cloves garlic (minced)
1 C. chopped celery
½ C. chopped carrots
¼ C. chopped parsley
1½ tsp. salt
½ tsp. pepper
1 tsp. nutmeg
1 tsp. oregano
1 tsp. basil
1 bay leaf

Place beans in large kettle and add 6 to 8 C. hot water. Bring to boil and boil for 2 minutes. Remove from heat, cover and let stand for 1 hour. Drain and add 2 quarts of cold water and hock. Bring to boil and simmer for 1½ hours. Stir in remaining ingredients and simmer for 20 to 30 minutes until beans are tender. Remove hock and trim off meat and return to soup. Note: Do not add salt if cured pork is used.

Ham-Potato-Cheese Chowder

2 medium potatoes (diced, 2 C.)
1 C. water
1 C. chopped onion
3 T. butter
3½ T. flour
Dash of pepper & salt
3 C. milk
1½ C. small cubed ham
1½ C. (6 oz.) sharp Cheddar cheese

Cook potato in water. Drain, reserving liquid and adding enough water to make 1 cup. Cook onion in butter until tender. Blend in flour, salt, and pepper. Add milk and potato water. Cook until mixture bubbles, stirring constantly. Add ham, potato, and cheese; bring up to heat.

Granny Drury's Fish Chowder

1/2 lb. bacon, cut in 1/2" squares
3 or 4 potatoes
2 or 3 onions
Fresh fish
Whole milk

Render bacon; take out and put aside. Cook onions and potatoes in bacon fat. Cook fish in 1 to 2 cups of water. Add all fish and water to bacon fat, onions and potatoes. Add milk as you want. Salt and pepper to taste. Serve hot and sprinkled with bacon pieces.

WILD RICE SOUP

6 slices bacon (cut up)
1 medium onion (chopped)
2 C. cooked wild rice
1 pt. Half and Half
2 medium potatoes (grated)
1 C. chopped celery
2 C. milk
2 cans chicken broth
1 T. (heaping) cornstarch
1 grated carrot
Handful of chives

Mix together and heat. Cook until vegetables are done. Works good in a crock pot on low for about 4 hours.

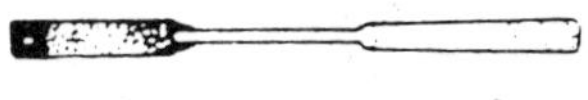

WILD RICE SOUP

2 cans cream of potato soup
12 slices bacon
4 T. chopped onion
1½-2 C. cooked wild rice
2 pints Half and Half
2 C. shredded American or cheddar cheese

Saute onion in bacon drippings. Crumble bacon. Heat all ingredients, but cheese, stirring constanlty. Add cheese. Options: may add celery, mushrooms, etc. If too thick, add 1 soup can of milk and water to desired consistency.

BEAN SOUP

1 C. dry beans
6 C. water
Meaty ham bone
1 small onion (chopped)
Salt and pepper

Boil gently for 2 hours in covered kettle or until beans are soft. Remove bone and cut off meat. Return meat to soup. Season soup to taste and reheat it.

SALADS

Potato-Ham Salad

4 large boiling potatoes
1 (10 oz.) can cond. consomme'
1 clove garlic (whole)
¼ C. sliced green onion
¼ C. chopped fresh parsley or
1 T. minced fresh tarragon
1 C. ham (diced)
½ C. freshly grated Parmesan cheese

Pare the potatoes and quarter. Cook in consomme' with garlic until just tender. Drain, reserving broth for soup or gravy. Dice potatoes; add ham and green onion. Combine dressing ingredients; drizzle over potatoes, tossing gently. Sprinkle with cheese and parsley. Serve at room temperature.

DRESSING:

3 T. white wine vinegar or tarragon vinegar
2 T. olive oil
½ tsp. Dijon-style mustard
¼ tsp. salt (optional)

This will serve 4.

Hot Spinach Salad

1 lb. spinach
½ lb. vertically sliced mushrooms
3 hard-cooked eggs (chopped)
6 slices bacon (cooked & crumbled)
½ C. salad oil
3 T. bacon fat
¼ C. ketchup
½ medium chopped onion
¼ C. cider vinegar
1 T. Worcestershire sauce
2 T. sugar

Wash spinach thoroughly and pull off steams. Dry leaves well on paper towel and tear into bite-sized pieces. Arrange in a bowl with mushroom, bacon, and eggs. In a skillet, combine remaining ingredients and heat to a simmer. Pour hot dressing over salad. Gently toss and serve at once.

Vegetable Macaroni Ham Salad

1 lb. macaroni (cooked)
1 large chopped green pepper
1 chopped onion
4 carrots (shredded)

Celery (sliced)
Cheese (chunked)
Ham (chunked)

Combine all. Mix dressing of 1 can Eagle Brand milk, 1 C. of vinegar, 1 C. sugar, 2 C. mayonnaise, and 1¼ tsp. pepper, to taste. Combine all together.

Wild Rice and Raisin Salad

½ C. wild rice
½ C. pecan halves (20 large)
½ lb. lean ham
¼ tsp. pepper
¾ C. golden raisins
(soaked in hot water & drained)

½ C. thinly sliced green onions
⅓ C. olive oil
¼ C. rice wine vinegar
Lettuce cups

Generously cover rice with water in 3-quart sauce pot. Turn into a strainer to drain; repeat several times to wash the rice thoroughly. Return rice to sauce pot. Add 2 quarts water, heat to boil, cover and boil gently, without stirring, 40 to 50 minutes until tender and each grain has opened. Have extra boiling water in hand to add toward the end of cooking so that the rice is covered with boiling water. Rinse with hot running water, draining well. Spread pecan halves in single layer in shallow baking pan. Bake at preheated 350° oven for 10 minutes or until toasted. Slice ham into 1/8 to ¼-inch wide and 1-inch long strips. Stir together rice, ham, raisins, and green onions in large bowl. Whisk together olive oil, vinegar, and pepper in small bowl. Pour over rice mixture and toss. Cover and chill. At serving time, turn into lettuce cups. Garnish with pecans. Rice can be cooked according to package directions.

SPINACH SALAD

1 bunch fresh spinach
1 medium onion
Crispy bacon bits
½ C. vinegar
½ C. sugar
¼ C. salad oil
2 hard boiled eggs (opt.)

Wash spinach, drain. Tear in smaller pieces. Cut up onion in small pieces. Add about 1 C. bacon bits. Combine vinegar, sugar, and oil. Shake well and pour over spinach. Hard boiled eggs are optional. Serve immediately.

BROCCOLI SALAD

1 C. fresh chopped broccoli
1 medium red onion
12-14 slices bacon (fried and crumbled)

Add 1 C. real mayonnaise, 2 T. sugar, 2 T. vinegar. Pour over broccoli; mix and chill overnight.

BROCCOLI DELIGHT SALAD

1 large bunch fresh broccoli
¼ C. diced onion
1 C. raisins
1 C. sunflower seeds
10 strips bacon (fried and diced)

DRESSING:
½ C. mayonnaise
1 T. vinegar
3-4 T. sugar

Place diced, well drained broccoli in large bowl. Add raisins, onion, sunflower seeds and bacon. Mix dressing ingredients. Pour over salad and toss well. Chill for ½ hour.

OVERNIGHT SALAD

1 head lettuce (washed and drained well)
1 small red onion

½ head cauliflower (washed and dried and cut into bits)
1 lb. bacon (fried crisp)

1 C. Hellmann's real mayonnaise
1 small can Parmesan cheese

¼ C. sugar

All ingredients should be dry or salad will be soupy. Cut onion into rings or chop. Layer in serving bowl and make dressing but do not mix until ready to serve. To make dressing, just blend all 3 ingredients well. This may be made the night before and stored in refrigerator in Tupperware or airtight container, but Do Not toss until ready to serve.

HAM SALAD

½-¾ lb. bologna
8 oz. family loaf
Sweet pickle relish and juice
Miracle Whip
8 oz. spiced ham
2-3 hard boiled eggs
Mustard

Grind and mix meat. Mix pickle juice, sugar, mustard, and Miracle Whip. Add all ingredients together. Chop eggs and add. Mix well.

Spinach Salad

2 lb. fresh spinach
10 slices bacon
2 T. vegetable oil
1/3 c. chopped onion
3 T. salad vinegar
1 tsp. sorghum
1/2 tsp. salt
1/8 tsp. pepper
1 hard-boiled egg, peeled & sliced

Wash spinach, discarding any leaves that are not fresh. Cook in a large saucepan with the water that clings to the leaves, until tender, about 8 to 10 minutes. Drain. While spinach is cooking, fry the bacon. When crisp, drain on paper towels and crumble when cool. Discard the bacon grease, wipe the skillet with a paper towel and add the vegetable oil. Sauté the onion until soft. Blend the vinegar, sorghum, salt and pepper in the sautéed onion. Add the spinach and bacon; toss. Place in bowl and garnish with egg slices. Serves 6.

Spinach Salad Divine

- 1 lb. spinach, washed & torn into pieces
- 1 lb. can bean sprouts, chilled & drained
- 10 slices bacon, cooked & crumbled
- 3 hard-boiled eggs, peeled & chopped
- 1/2 tsp. salt
- 3 T. ketchup
- 1/4 c. sorghum
- 2 T. salad vinegar
- 1/2 tsp. instant minced onion
- 1/2 tsp. Worcestershire sauce
- 1/2 tsp. salt
- 1/2 c. salad oil

Combine the spinach, bean sprouts, bacon and eggs in a salad bowl. Sprinkle with 1/2 teaspoon salt. In a small mixing bowl, combine the ketchup, sorghum, vinegar, onion, Worcestershire sauce, salt and salad oil. Stir until blended. To serve, sprinkle the dressing over the spinach. Serves 8 to 10.

Skillet Potato Salad

10 slices bacon
1/4 c. vegetable oil
1/2 c. chopped celery
1/2 c. chopped onion
3 T. sorghum
3 T. flour
1 1/2 tsp. salt
1/2 tsp. celery seed
1/4 tsp. pepper
1/3 c. salad vinegar
1/2 c. water
5 c. potatoes, cooked & cubed

Fry bacon until crisp, drain on paper towels. Discard bacon grease and wipe skillet clean. Heat vegetable oil in a large, heavy skillet. Add celery and cook until tender-crisp. Add onion and cook 2 minutes longer. Add sorghum, flour, salt, celery seeds and pepper to celery and onion mixture. Stir well. Add vinegar and water, stirring until smooth. Bring to a boil and add potatoes and bacon. Mix thoroughly, heat until potatoes are hot. Serves 6.

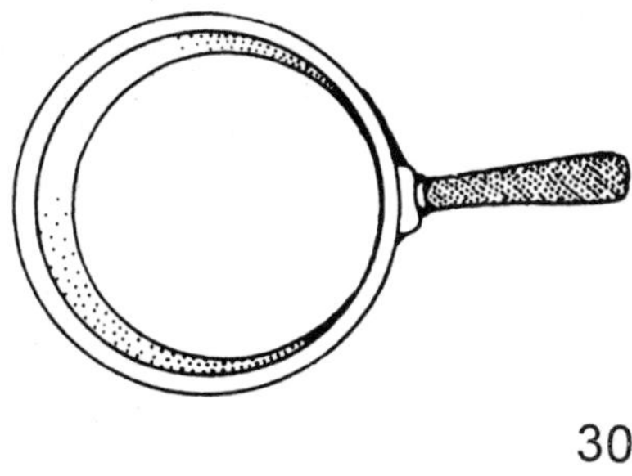

Dutch-Style Spinach Salad

2 qt. spinach, washed & torn
4 green onions, chopped
5 slices bacon
3 T. vegetable oil
3 T. flour
3 T. sorghum
1 tsp. salt
1/4 tsp. pepper
1 1/2 c. hot water
3 T. salad vinegar
2 hard-boiled eggs, peeled & chopped

Place spinach and onions in a salad bowl. Fry the bacon until crisp. Drain on paper towels. Discard bacon grease and rub skillet with a clean paper towel. Put vegetable oil in skillet and heat over medium heat. Add flour and blend. Stir in sorghum, salt, pepper and hot water. Cook, stirring all the while, until mixture comes to a boil. Stir in vinegar. Pour vinegar mixture over spinach and onions. Add eggs and toss. Top with crumbled bacon. Serve immediately. Makes 6 servings.

SHOESTRING POTATO SALAD

1 C. celery (diced)
2 boiled eggs (cut-up)
1 C. chicken, turkey, tuna or ham
1 C. grated carrots
1 small onion (diced or minced)
1 C. Miracle Whip
Salt, pepper & garlic powder, to taste
1 small can shoestring potatoes

Mix all ingredients, except potatoes. Add potatoes when ready to serve.

HAM SALAD

Cook ham and grind. Grind Velveeta cheese and peppers. Mix this with ham and add salad dressing till the meat is good and moist. The amount of cheese and peppers depends on how much ham you have and also how well you like cheese and peppers.

MAIN DISHES

Main Dishes

OVERNIGHT CASSEROLE

1 ¾ C. uncooked macaroni
2 C. chicken, turkey or ham (cooked)
2 C. mushroom soup
Pimento may be added
½ lb. Velveeta cheese (cubed)
3 hard cooked eggs
2 C. milk

Mix all ingredients into a 3-qt. casserole or 9x13-inch pan. Cover and place in refrigerator overnight. Next day allow 1 hour to come to room temperature. Bake uncovered at 350° for 1 hour and 15 minutes.

SWEET AND SOUR PORK CHOPS

4 rib pork chops
Vegetable oil
Salt
Pepper

1 (8 oz.) can pineapple chunks and juice
⅓ C. Heinz 57 sauce
1 medium green pepper

In skillet brown 4 rib pork chops, ¾-inch thick, in vegetable oil. Drain fat. Season chops with salt and pepper. Combine 1 (8 oz.) can pineapple chunks and juice with ⅓ C. Heinz 57 sauce. Pour over chops. Cover, simmer 45 minutes or until chops are tender. Add 1 medium green pepper (cut into strips). Cover, simmer 15-20 minutes or until pepper is tender. Thicken sauce with cornstarch-water mixture if desired. Makes 4 servings.

CRAZY BEANS

½ lb. bacon (fried and diced)
½ lb. ground beef
1 small onion
½ C. white sugar
½ C. brown sugar

¼ C. catsup
1 (No. 2) can drained pork and beans
1 (No. 2) can butter beans
1 (No. 2) can kidney beans

Brown diced bacon. Add ground beef and chopped onion to browned bacon. When cooked, remove excess fat. Add rest of ingredients. Bake at 350° for 1 hour.

THREE BEAN BAKE

1 lb. can pork and beans
1 lb. can Northern beans
1 lb. can kidney beans (drained)
½ C. brown sugar
1 tsp. Worcestershire sauce
1 medium onion (chopped)
¼ lb. sharp cheddar cheese (cubed)
⅓ C. catsup
4 slices bacon (cut up)

Brown bacon and onion. Mix with all other ingredients. Bake at 350° for 1 hour.

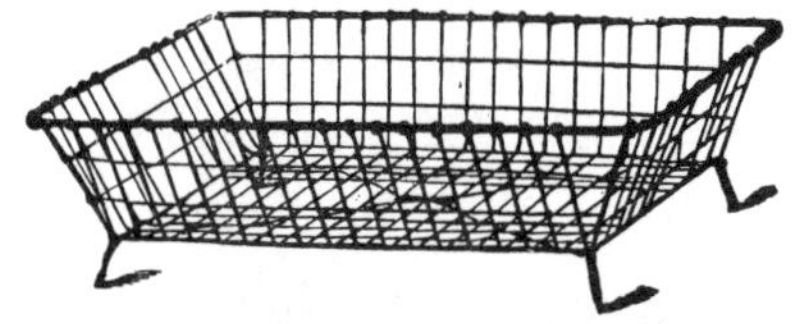

SOUPER BEEF-N-TATERS

1½ lbs. ground beef or pork
1 egg
Salt and pepper to taste
1 small onion (chopped)
¼ tsp. oregano
¼ tsp. marjoram
¼ tsp. thyme
1 can cream of mushroom or celery soup
½ can milk
2 lb. bag Tater Tots

Brown meat, egg and onion; drain 5 minutes. Add ½ can soup and seasonings. Cook 5 minutes more on Full Power. Top with Tater Tots, spread out even. Mix other ½ can of soup and ½ can milk, pour over top of taters. Cook until taters are done about 5 minutes on Full Power, covered with waxed paper, uncovered for 2 minutes. Let set 1 minute. Serve. May add frozen peas after meat is cooked and stir.

CROCK POT HAM BALLS

1 lb. ham loaf mixture
  (½ ground ham, ¼ ground pork,
  ¼ ground round)
Pepper
1 small egg
1 C. bread crumbs
½ C. milk

SAUCE:
½ C. brown sugar
½ tsp. mustard
½ C. water
¼ C. cider vinegar

Shape into 11 or 12 balls about 2-inches in diameter. Place on broiler pan. Brown 15-30 minutes in 400° oven. Place ham balls in crock pot. Heat sauce ingredients until syrupy. Pour over ham balls. Cook on low setting for 6 hours. Baste occasionally.

INDIVIDUAL HAM LOAF

1 ½ lbs. ground beef
1 ½ lbs. ground ham
1 ½ C. cracker crumbs
3 eggs (beaten)
1 C. milk

TOPPING:
¾ C. brown sugar
1 T. mustard
1 C. ketchup

Mix first 5 ingredients. Make into mini loaves. Put into baking dish. Mix brown sugar, ketchup and mustard. Drizzle on ham loaves. Bake 1 hour at 350°.

CHOUCROUTE GARNI

(Excellent for Company)

1 medium onion (sliced)
1 T. fat
2 lbs. spare ribs (cut in rib portions) or 1 smoked pork chop per person or 1-2 lbs. smoked shoulder roll (cut in ¾-inch slices)
2-3 large cans sauerkraut (drained and rinsed)
2 cooking apples (peeled, cored, or sliced)
2 T. packed brown sugar
4 whole cloves
2 small cloves garlic (minced)
1 bay leaf
½ tsp. pepper
1½ C. Rhine wine
1 lb. sausage (Polish, Bratwurst, brockwurst, or knackwurst, thuringer or weiners) (use combination of these or one of your choice)
Boiled potatoes

In Dutch oven brown onion in fat, leave in bottom of pan and add all pork, except the sausage. In large bowl stir together sauerkraut, apples, brown sugar, cloves, garlic, bay leaves and pepper. Spoon over meats. Pour wine over all. Cover and bake at 350° for 2½ hours. Last 45 minutes of baking time, add sausage and potatoes, continue to cook at end of time. Spoon out sauerkraut and mound on platter. Arrange meats around kraut. This dish is a little different way of using kraut. Another meal in one. All you need is a salad to go with it.

COUNTRY RIBS AND SAUERKRAUT BAKE

5-6 ribs (country)
1 large can sauerkraut
2 small cans stew tomatoes with peppers and onions in them
A little salt and pepper
½ C. rice
Sugar to taste to take away some of the tart

Brown the ribs. Pressure cook for 1 hour, with a little water added. Put all other ingredients in 9x13-inch pan. Rinse sauerkraut first in water. Drain. Mix all together and place ribs on top. Pour all of the juice from pressure cooker overall. Bake for 45 minutes to 1 hour at 325°.

MEN'S DELIGHT

1 lb. ground chuck
1 lb. Velveeta cheese
2 loaves party rye bread
1 lb. pork sausage
1 T. garlic salt

Brown ground chuck and pork sausage; drain well. Cube cheese and mix with the meat over low heat until cheese melts; add garlic salt. Brown one side of the bread; turn over and put 1 T. (generous) meat mixture on each slice. Brown under broiler. Can be made ahead and frozen.

EGG CASSEROLE

18 eggs
5 C. milk
1 tsp. pepper
2 tsp. salt
2 tsp. Worcestershire sauce
2 tsp. dry mustard
16 slices bread (cubed)
3 C. diced ham
4 C. shredded cheese

Place bread on bottom of 9x13-inch pan. Put ham and cheese on top of bread and egg mixture. Bake at 350° for 1 hour.

HOT PIZZA DISH

1 lb. ground beef or pork
⅓ C. chopped green pepper
½ C. chopped onion
1 (16 oz.) can pizza or tomato sauce
2 C. (5 oz.) dry, uncooked noodles
1 (4 oz.) can mushrooms (drained)
8 oz. pepperoni (minced)
1 C. water
1 C. (4 oz.) grated mozzarella cheese
1 T. pizza seasoning (if using tomato sauce)

Cook beef, green pepper and onion on Full Power for 5-6 minutes or brown on stove top until done. Drain. Add the remainder of ingredients, except cheese. Cook, covered, on Full Power for 15-17 minutes. Stir 2-3 times. Noodles will soften and cook absorbing the extra moisture. Top with mozzarella cheese after casserole is cooked. Let stand 5-10 minutes, covered, before serving. (I use large square casserole pan.)

BREAKFAST CASSEROLE

3 C. cubed bread
3 C. cubed ham
3 C. shredded cheddar cheese
3 T. flour
1 T. dry mustard
¼ C. melted butter
8 eggs
2 C. milk

Layer bread, ham and cheese in 9x13-inch buttered pan. Beat eggs and milk together. Add butter. Mix flour and dry mustard together. Sprinkle flour mixture over bread, ham and cheese. Pour egg mixture over layers. Bake at 350° for 1 hour. This can be prepared the night before and baked in the morning.

CROCK O'BEANS

½ lb. bacon (cut up)
½ lb. hamburger
½ lb. minced ham (cut up)
½ C. white sugar
½ C. brown sugar
2 T. vinegar
2 T. dry mustard
½ C. catsup
1 can red beans
1 can pork and beans
1 can lima beans (drained)

Brown bacon, hamburger and ham. Put in crock pot and add other ingredients. Cook at least 1 hour.

MEAT BALLS

1½ lbs. hamburger
1½ lbs. sausage
3 eggs
⅓ C. chopped onion
1 pt. finely ground bread crumbs
1½ tsp. salt
1½ tsp. pepper
½ C. milk
½ can cream of mushroom soup

Mix all ingredients. Roll in 3-inch balls and fry. Put in casserole dish and pour the rest of the mushroom soup plus one more can of mushroom soup diluted with 1 can of water. Bake in a covered dish at 350° for 1 hour.

GLORIA'S QUICK CASSEROLE

1 flat can chunk ham
12 oz. medium width noodles (cooked)
½ bag frozen California mixed vegetables (cooked and drained)
1 can cream of chicken soup
1 can cream of celery soup
1 C. shredded cheddar cheese
1 (2.8 oz.) can French-fried onion rings

Mix together cooked and drained noodles, diced ham, cooked and drained California mixed vegetables, cream of chicken soup and cream of celery soups, ½ can French-fried onion rings, ½ C. cheese. Place in greased 3-qt. casserole and bake at 350° for 45 minutes. Top with rest of cheese and other half can of onion rings. Return to oven for about 5-7 minutes more.

Rabbit Or Squirrel Stew

Rabbit (or squirrel)
1 qt. water
3-4 slices bacon
3 potatoes (chopped)
1 small can tomatoes
2 beef bouillon cubes
1 C. whole grain corn
1 large onion (chopped)
Salt and pepper

Place water in a stew pan, along with cut up rabbit (or squirrel). Cut up bacon and add. Let simmer until meat is tender, then all remainder of ingredients. Salt and pepper well. Let stew until potatoes are tender, then serve. Good with corn bread.

STUFFED MUSHROOMS

1 lb. mushrooms (fresh)
1 lb. bacon
1½ lbs. Monterey Jack cheese (2-3 C.)

Clean and remove stems from mushrooms; chop stems. Brown bacon until crisp. Leave 2 T. fat in pan. Saute mushroom stems. Add jack cheese and stir until melted. Add broken up bacon bits to this cheese mixture and stir well to blend. Stuff mushrooms with this mixture. Refrigerate. When ready to serve, place in 350° oven for about 20 minutes. Bake covered until last few minutes. These are our favorite hors d'oeuvres. Yummy! Yummy!

SURPRISE TACO PIE

1 lb. ground beef
1 lb. ground pork
1 pkg. taco seasoning mix
1 C. tomato sauce (or taco sauce)
3 eggs
1 ½ C. milk
¾ C. Bisquick
1 ½ C. shredded Monterey Jack cheese
2 tomatoes (thinly sliced)

Cook meat and onion in casserole dish covered with paper towel, on full power for 7-9 minutes or brown on stove. Stir with a fork several times. Drain and stir in seasoning and sauce. Spread in a 10-inch pie plate or quiche dish or square casserole dish. Beat milk, baking mix and eggs until smooth, 15 seconds in blender on high or 1 minute. Pour over meat. Cook in microwave 7-8 minutes on Full Power, turn halfway through cooking time. Sprinkle with cheese. Top with tomatoes. Return to microwave and cook on Full Power for 2-3 minutes. Cool 5 minutes. Serve with sour cream, chopped tomatoes and shredded lettuce, if desired. Good potluck dish. Can be baked in oven for 20 minutes at 350°. Top with cheese and tomatoes and bake 5 more minutes. (I use square casserole dish.)

MEAL IN A CASSEROLE

4 pork chops
1 T. fat
Salt & pepper
4 C. cooked noodles
2 T. chopped onions
3 tsp. chopped green pepper
1 can tomato soup

Brown chops in 1 T. fat and season. Put noodles in casserole and sprinkle onion and peppers over noodles. Pour tomato soup over this. Lastly place browned pork chops on top. Bake at 350° for 45 minutes.

PREACHER'S COMIN' PORK CHOPS

4 pork chops
½ C. soy sauce
¼ C. sugar
½ tsp. garlic powder
½ tsp. salt
1 tsp. ginger

Mix and pour over chops. Marinate for 4 to 8 hours, turning occasionally. Double recipe for Iowa chops. Best when barbecued.

HAM AND RICE CASSEROLE

1 ½ C. cubed ham (already baked)
1 C. frozen peas (optional)
2 T. chopped green pepper (optional)
2 T. chopped parsley (less if used dry)
1 C. grated cheddar cheese
1 C. uncooked Minute Rice

3 eggs
1 ½ C. scalded milk
¼ tsp. salt
Mushroom soup
½ C. milk

Scald milk and let set for a few minutes. Beat eggs (for a few seconds) in a large bowl. Add other ingredients and mix together. Pour into greased casserole dish. Bake at 350° for 1 hour. (You may want to cover for part of baking time.)

For Sauce: Heat 1 can mushroom soup and ½ C. milk. Pour some over baked dish. Serve rest as a sauce.

RICE 'N PEPPER

3 or 4 strips of bacon with the drippings
1 C. rice (uncooked)
1 small onion (chopped)
½ green pepper (diced)
2 tsp. salt
2 tsp. chili powder (or less)
1 C. tomatoes or juice
2 C. water

Fry the bacon and break into pieces. Add rest of ingredients and cover tightly. Simmer slowly for about 20 minutes or until rice is done. If rice becomes too dry add more juice or water as needed. This may be baked in a covered casserole for 40 to 50 minutes or until done in 350° oven.

Optional: Mushrooms may be added. Hamburger may be substituted for the bacon, if desired.

JAMBALAYA

3 slices bacon
½ C. uncooked long grain rice
1 medium onion (chopped)
1 (13 oz.) can chicken broth (1 ¾ C.)
1 (8 oz.) can tomato sauce
2 C. cubed & cooked chicken
1 C. fully cooked ham (cubed)
½ tsp. salt & dash ground pepper

In skillet cook bacon; drain, crumble and set aside. Add rice and onion to drippings and cook until golden, stirring frequently; reduce heat. Add chicken broth, tomato sauce, chicken, ham, salt and pepper. Cover and simmer til rice is tender, about 25 minutes, adding more water if necessary. Serves 6.

RIGATONI CASSEROLE

1 lb. Italian sausage
8 oz. pkg. rigatoni
12 oz. pizza sauce
8 oz. mozzarella cheese

Brown meat. Prepare pasta according to package directions. Stir together meat, pizza sauce, and pasta. Pour into a greased 9x13-inch pan. Sprinkle with cheese. Cover; bake at 350° for 30 minutes. Uncover, bake 10-15 minutes more.

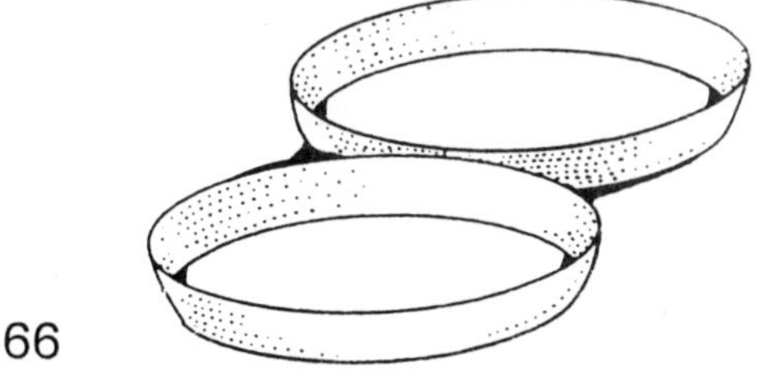

SOUTHERN PORK CHOPS

Brown 6 center cut pork chops in 2 T. oil in a skillet. Top each browned chop with ¼ T. lemon juice, 1 slice (thick) onion and 1 slice green pepper. Top each chop generously with catsup. Add 1 can tomato sauce (8 oz.) and 1 can water. Sprinkle ¾ C. (packed) brown sugar over top. Set skillet for 340° for 45 minutes or until tender.

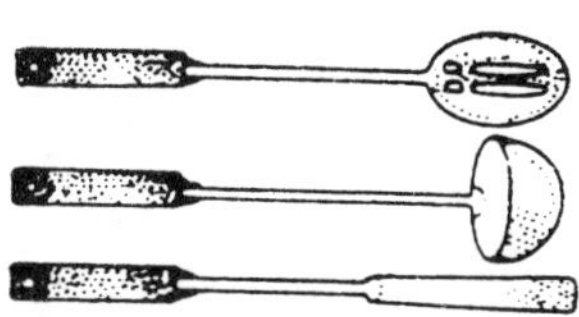

CROCK POT ROAST PORK

4 lb. lean pork roast
1½ C. water
½ C. wine
1 tsp. salt
1 tsp. thyme
1 tsp. ground sage
1 clove garlic

Put roast in crock pot. Mix ingredients together and pour over roast. Cook low 4-5 hours.

RICE AND HAM CASSEROLE

1 box Uncle Ben's wild long grain rice (cooked)
20 oz. broccoli (precooked for 3 minutes)
2 C. chopped ham
1 C. shredded cheddar cheese

MIX TOGETHER:
1 can celery soup
1 tsp. mustard
1 C. mayonnaise

Lay rice in bottom of greased 9x13-inch pan. Layer broccoli, ham and shredded cheese on top rice. Spread your celery soup, mayonnaise and mustard mixture on top of ham and rice. Top with ½ C. Parmesan cheese. Bake uncovered at 350° oven for 40-45 minutes.

CHOW MEIN

1 1/4 lb. veal
1 1/4 lb. pork
1 large onion (chopped)
1 bunch celery
1 can bean sprouts (do not drain)
1 can chow mein vegetables
(do not drain)

1 can mushrooms
1 can water chestnuts
1 can bamboo shoots
2 T. soy sauce
2 T. flour
Chow mein noodles or rice

Cut veal and pork in cubes and sear. When brown add onions and fry. Boil chopped celery. Add celery water, bean sprouts and chow mein vegetables, water, and all to meat. Let cook 1 hour. Add mushrooms, water chestnuts, and bamboo shoots. Warm through. Thicken last with soy sauce and flour. Serve on chow mein noodles or rice.

ITALIAN MEAT LOAF

1½ lbs. ground beef
1 egg
¾ C. cracker crumbs
2 (8 oz. ea.) cans tomato sauce
1 tsp. salt
½ C. chopped onion
½ tsp. oregano (crushed)
1/8 tsp. pepper
2 C. shredded mozzarella

Combine meat, eggs, crackers, onion, and seasonings. Put ½ C. tomato sauce in meat mixture. Pat out and sprinkle with cheese. Roll and seal edges. Put in shallow dish. Bake at 350° for 1 hour. Drain and add rest of sauce. Bake for 15 minutes more.

HAM AND NOODLE CASSEROLE

1 small pkg. noodles
2 C. ground ham
1 can cream of mushroom soup
  or cream of chicken soup

1 C. milk
½ C. potato chip crumbs
1 small can mushrooms (opt.)

Cook noodles in salted water until tender; drain. Put noodles, ham, and soup in buttered caserole dish, alternating the layers until all are used. Pour milk on top and over this the potato chips. Bake at 350° for about 45 minutes.

HAM BALLS

4 lbs. ham
1 lb. sausage
2 lbs. hamburger
6 eggs
6 C. graham cracker crumbs
4 C. milk

SAUCE:
1 can tomato soup
1 C. brown sugar
½ C. vinegar
1 T. dry mustard

Mix meats, eggs, crumbs, and milk together. Shape in balls, about ½ C. each. Bake at 350° about ½ hour. Put your mixed sauce on top each ham ball, return to oven. Bake another ¾-1 hour. Makes about 36 ham balls.

WIENIE BAKE

5 C. diced boiled potatoes
2 C. drained sauerkraut
1 lb. sliced all-beef weiners
(cut fine with scissors)
1 can cream of mushroom soup
½ C. mayonnaise

3 rounded T. minced fresh
onion
2 T. caraway seed
1½ tsp. Italian seasoning
¼ tsp. garlic powder or less

Mix and put in buttered casserole. Cover with crushed potato chips or seasoned bread crumbs. Bake at 350° for 45 minutes. Serves 9 or 10.

HAM LOAF

2 lb. lean ground ham
1 lb. lean ground fresh pork
2 eggs
1 C. cracker crumbs
Milk
½ C. brown sugar
2 tsp. salad mustard
Chopped onions

Mix brown sugar, eggs, and mustard. Add to meat and blend in. Mix onion and cracker crumbs. Form into loaf and put in loaf pan. Pour milk over to almost cover.

HAM AND CHEESE TOWERS

¼ C. margarine
¼ C. flour
1½ C. milk
1 chicken cube
½ C. hot water
2 oz. grated sharp American cheese

1 tsp. prepared mustard
1 T. Worcestershire sauce
1½ C. chopped ham
⅓ C. chopped olives
1 small jar pimentos (chopped)
2 T. parsley flakes

Combine margarine, flour, and milk to make white sauce. Then add chicken cube that has been dissolved in hot water. Combine remaining ingredients and add to white sauce. Simmer 15-20 minutes. May be thickened with cornstarch if too thin. Serve over patty shells. Mixture freezes well and can be made ahead of time.

Maidrites Oink

1½ lbs. ground pork (browned)
½ C. ketchup
¼ C. BBQ sauce
½ tsp. Worcestershire sauce
2 T. brown sugar
¾ of a tube of Ritz crackers (crushed)

Combine all ingredients and simmer in fry pan for 15-30 minutes. The Ritz crackers make them stick together and not crumble.

Pork Sausage 'N' Wild Rice Casserole

¾ C. wild rice or Uncle Ben's Minute Rice
1 lb. lean pork
1 (8 oz.) can mushrooms
1 onion (chopped)
4 T. all-purpose flour
½ C. cream or Half & Half
1 can chicken broth
1/8 tsp. thyme
¼ tsp. oregano
1/8 tsp. margarine
1½ tsp. salt
½ C. slivered almonds (optional)

Cook rice according to directions on package. Fry pork, sausage, crumble, and drain off fat. Saute onions. Mix flour and stir in cream, salt, thyme, oregano, margarine, slivered almonds, and mushrooms. Mix in the cooked rice, and chicken broth. Bake at 350° for 40 to 45 minutes.

Breakfast Buns

5 hamburger buns
3 T. margarine
5 eggs
¼ C. milk
½ C. diced ham or grated cheese

Spread about 1 tsp. magarine on each bun half and brown in skillet; set aside. Beat eggs and milk with a fork. Pour into preheated non-stick or lightly oiled pan. Stir while cooking until eggs set. Put heaping tablespoon of eggs on each bun half. Sprinkle cheese or ham on top.

SILVER DOLLAR STEAKS

1 lb. 75-80 percent lean ground pork
1 tsp. salt
¼ tsp. pepper
1 egg
¼ C. bread crumbs
1 T. onion flakes
1 T. dried mixed vegetables (opt.)
1 can cream of chicken soup

Beat egg; add remaining ingredients except soup and vegetables. Shape into 4 flattened steaks. Pour soup over steaks. Sprinkle dried mixed vegetables on top of soup. Bake 1 hour at 350°. Serves 4. Variation: Substitute 1 can of any cream soup for chicken soup.

SWEET SOUR PORK

1 ½ lb. pork shoulder
2 T. oil
½ C. water
15½-oz. can pineapple chunks
2 T. cornstarch
¼ C. brown sugar
⅓ C. vinegar
1 T. soy sauce
¾ green pepper
¼ C. thinly sliced onion
½ tsp. salt

Brown pork cubed in hot skillet. Add water and simmer covered 1 hour until tender. Drain pineapple, reserving juice. Add water if necessary to make 1 C. Combine cornstarch, salt and brown sugar. Blend in vinegar; stir in reserved pineapple juice and soy sauce. Cook stirring constantly until thickened and bubbly. Pour sauce over hot pork and let stand 10 minutes. Add green pepper, onion and pineapple chunks. Simmer covered 2-3 minutes or until vegetables are tender. Serve over cooked rice. Serves 4.

Ham and Cheese Goodies

¼ C. onions (chopped)
¼ C. green pepper (chopped)
1 T. margarine
12 slices bread (cubed with crust on)
6 ozs. Swiss cheese (grated)
8 ozs. Cheddar cheese (grated)
½ C. mushrooms (drained)
12 ozs. ham (diced)
6 eggs
3 C. milk
¼ tsp. salt
½ tsp. dry mustard

Suate onions and peppers in margarine. In greased 9x13-inch pan; add onions, peppers, bread, cheese, mushrooms, and ham. Mix together. In mixing bowl, beat with wire whip until well blended the eggs, milk, salt, and dry mustard. Pour over bread mixture. Cover with Saran wrap and refrigerate overnight. Bake at 325° for 30 to 40 minutes or until knife inserted in middle of product comes out clean. Let stand 10 minutes after pulling from oven before cutting. Makes 12 to 15 servings.

HAM BALLS

1 ¼ lbs. ground smoked ham
1 lb. ground lean pork
½ lb. ground beef
2 eggs
1 ½ C. crushed graham crackers
1 C. milk

SAUCE:

1 can tomato soup
¼ C. vinegar
1 C. brown sugar
1 tsp. dry mustard

Mix ingredients well and form into small balls. Mix the sauce ingredients and pour over meatballs. Put foil on brownie pan and bake at 350° for 1 hour or 1 ½ hours.

CHEESE AND BACON OVEN OMELET

12 slices of bacon
8 eggs (beaten)
6 slices cheese
1 C. milk

Cook bacon and drain, curl 1 slice, chop 4 slices, and leave others whole. Arrange cheese in bottom of buttered 9-inch pie pan. Beat together eggs and milk. Add chopped bacon, Pour over cheese and bake for 30 minutes in 350° oven. Arrange whole bacon on top around curl. Bake 10 minutes longer. Let stand 5 minutes before cutting.

Hog Heaven Ham Balls

2½ lbs. ground smoked ham
3 lbs. ground beef
4 eggs
2 to 3 C. crushed graham crackers
1 C. milk

SAUCE:
2 cans tomato soup
¾ C. vinegar
2¼ C. brown sugar
2 tsp. dry mustard

Combine ground meats, eggs, graham crackers, and milk. Mix well and shape into 1-inch balls (makes 100 to 150). Combine ingredients for sauce and pour over meatballs. Bake at 300° for 2 hours. Serve warm or cold. Will freeze well.

Ham and Broccoli Roll Ups

1 bunch fresh broccoli or
  1 (10 oz.) pkg. frozen spears
5 thin slices cooked ham
½ C. mayonnaise
3 T. flour

½ tsp. salt
1/8 tsp. pepper
1½ C. milk
⅓ C. grated Parmesan or Cheddar
Fine dry bread crumbs

Roll ham around broccoli spears. Place rolls in shallow casserole. In small saucepan, stir together mayonnaise, flour, salt, and pepper. Gradually stir in milk. Cook over low heat, stirring constantly until thickened. Add cheese, stirring until blended. Pour sauce over rolls. Sprinkle with bread crumbs. Broil 6 inches from source of heat for 2 minutes or until bubbly. Serves 5.

Ham and Asparagus

1 small can evaporated milk
2 C. cooked cubed ham
2 C. cooked rice
1 (10 oz.) pkg. asparagus spears
2 C. shredded Cheddar cheese
1 can cream of mushroom soup
3 T. chopped onion
½ C. cornflake crumbs
3 T. melted butter or margarine

Mix water with milk to make ¾ cup. Combine ham, rice, soup, onion, and cheese. Put ½ ham mixture in greased 13x9-inch pan. Put asparagus on top and spoon on rest of ham mixture. Mix cornflakes and butter; sprinkle on top. Bake at 375° for 25 to 30 minutes. Cooked chicken and broccoli can be substituted.

Egg and Sausage Casserole

1 lb. lean sausage
6 eggs
2 C. milk
1 tsp. salt
1 tsp. dry mustard
2 slices cubed bread
1 C. grated Cheddar cheese

Brown, drain, and crumble sausage. Beat eggs, milk, mustard, and salt; add bread, then cheese and sausage. Put in 7x11-inch baking dish or casserole. Refrigerate overnight. Next day, bake at 350° for 45 minutes. Allow to set for 5 minutes.

CREAMY HAM AND MACARONI BAKE

2 C. uncooked macaroni
2 T. oleo
3 T. flour
1 tsp. salt
1 tsp. parsley flakes
¾ tsp. dry mustard
¼ tsp. pepper
2 C. milk
2½ C. American cheese
2 C. diced ham
2 C. broccoli
1 C. sliced mushrooms
3 T. bread crumbs

Prepare macaroni according to directions and set aside. In large saucepan, melt oleo. Stir in flour, salt, parsley flakes, dry mustard, and pepper. Blend in milk. Cook, stirring constantly, until thick and bubbly. Add cheese; stir until melted. Add cooked macaroni, ham, broccoli, and mushrooms; mix well. Pour into buttered 2-qt. casserole. Sprinkle with bread crumbs. Bake at 350° for 30 minutes. Refrigerate leftovers. Makes 4-6 servings.

SWEDISH HAM BALLS

1½ lbs. ground cured ham
2 eggs
1 C. milk
½ C. vinegar
1 tsp. dry mustard
1½ lb. sausage
2 C. bread crumbs (3 slices)
½ C. water
1½ C. brown sugar

Mix ham, sausage, eggs, bread crumbs and milk. Make into balls. Mix remaining ingredients and pour over ham balls. Bake 2 hours at 325°. Double for company.

Rousin' Casserole

11 slices bread (trim crusts & cube)
1 lb. bulk sausage (brown & drain)
9 egg (well beaten)
3 C. milk
1½ tsp. salt and pepper
1 tsp. dry mustard
8 oz. shredded cheddar cheese
½ C. chopped pepper
¼ C. chopped onion

Mix all ingredients and pour into 9×13-inch pan. Bake at 350° for 1 hour or till done.

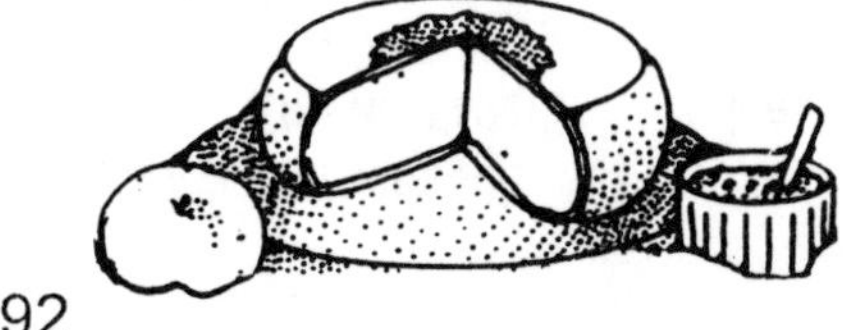

KOREAN SUN PORK

1 can pineapple chunks
3 T. soy sauce
1 T. cornstarch
1 tsp. white vinegar
½ tsp. hot red pepper flakes
1 lb. boneless pork roast
2 T. vegetable oil
2 large cloves garlic
2 T. minced ginger root
or 1 tsp. ground ginger
1 onion (quartered)
2 medium carrots (slivered)
1 green bell pepper (slivered)

Drain pineapple, reserve 3 T. juice. Mix reserved juice with water (½ C.); soy sauce, cornstarch, vinegar and pepper flakes; set aside. Cut pork in strips. In skillet, brown pork in hot oil. Add garlic and ginger; cook 1 minute. Add onion and carrots; cook 1 minute. Stir sauce; add to skillet with pineapple and bell pepper. Cook until sauce boils and thickens. Serves 4.

NORWEGIAN MEATBALLS

1 lb. ground beef
½ lb. pork sausage
½ C. dried bread crumbs
½ C. milk
1 egg

¾ C. onion
1 tsp. salt
1 tsp. sugar
¼ tsp. ginger, nutmeg and allspice

Soak bread crumbs in milk and combine with meat. Mix in egg, onion, salt, sugar and spices. Blend thoroughly. Shape into small balls. Brown in butter.

PUTZWUTZ

1 lb. sausage
1 diced green pepper
1 pkg. frozen corn
1 can tomato soup concentrate
1 lb. noodles (cooked)
1 lb. hamburger
1 diced onion
1 can sliced mushrooms
3 cans tomato sauce
1 lb. diced Velveeta cheese

Cook sausage, hamburger, green pepper, and onion until meat is cooked. Drain and combine remaining ingredients. Put in casserole dish and bake at 350° for 45 minutes. Makes 6-8 servings.

MACARONI HAM CASSEROLE

2 C. cooked elbow macaroni
1 ½ C. diced cooked ham
1 ½ C. diced cooked chicken
1 C. (4 oz.) shredded Swiss cheese
¾ C. sliced green olives
½ C. finely chopped onion
1 (8 oz.) carton commercial sour cream
¾ C. milk
¼ tsp. dry mustard
¼ tsp. pepper
¼ C. crushed potato chips

Combine first 6 ingredients; mix well. Combine sour cream, milk, dry mustard and pepper. Add to macaroni mixture and mix well. Spoon mixture into a lightly greased 2-qt. baking dish. Sprinkle with crushed potato chips. Bake at 350° for 25 minutes or until lightly browned. Yield: 6 servings.

PORK CHOP AND RICE CASSEROLE

Pork chops
¼ C. onion (chopped)
1 can mushroom soup
1 can mushrooms
1 C. rice
2 C. water

Brown pork chops in butter. Place chops into greased casserole dish. Brown mushrooms and onion in pan drippings. Add soup, rice, and water and heat through. Pour mixture over chops. Cover and bake for 325° for 45 minutes or unitl mixture has thickened.

Hot Times Barbeque Sauce

½ C. honey
¼ C. lemon juice
3-4 T. low sodium soy sauce
2 T. steak sauce (opt.)
1 tsp. dry mustard
1 tsp. ground ginger
1/8 tsp. ground cloves

Mix in small saucepan. Bring to a boil and remove from heat. Makes about 1 cup.

HAM BALLS

2½ lbs. ground ham
2 lbs. ground pork
1 lb. ground beef
3 C. crushed graham cracker
2 C. milk
3 eggs

SAUCE:
2 cans tomato soup
½ C. vinegar
2½ C. brown sugar
2 tsp. dry mustard

Mix first 6 ingredients well and form into balls (walnut size). Place in large pan at least 9x13-inch and cover with topping. (May wish to place in 2 pans.) Bake at 300° for 1½ hours.

Sauerkraut Casserole

5 strips bacon (fried and crumbled)
1 small onion (chopped)
1 C. brown sugar
2 lbs. sauerkraut
1 can tomatoes (drained)

Combine and bake 1 hour at 350°.

Sweet and Sour Sauerkraut

1 (No. 2½) can sauerkraut (drained)
1 large or 2 medium fresh tomatoes (sliced)
1 C. light brown packed brown sugar
1 small onion (chopped)
4 slices bacon (fried and crumbled)
4 T. bacon grease

Toss together all ingredients and bake at 350° for 1 hour.

DELICIOUS PORK CHOPS

4-5 pork chops
1 can cream of chicken soup
3 T. ketchup
1 T. Worcestershire sauce
1 medium onion (chopped)

Mix all ingredients into small bowl. Put chops in single layer in baking dish. Pour mixture over chops. Bake regular chops at 375° for 1 hour and large chops at 325° for 2 hours.

Ham Rolls

1½ lbs. ground ham
¾ lb. ground pork
¾ lb. ground beef
1½ C. crushed cracker crumbs
2 eggs (beaten)
1 C. milk
Dash of pepper

SAUCE:
½ C. vinegar
½ C. water
1½ C. brown sugar
1 T. dry mustard

Mix the first ingredients very well. Mix into egg shaped balls and place in baking dish. Make sauce and pour over balls. Cover casserole and bake at 350° for first hour, turn to 325° and bake 1 hour more, basting several times with sauce.

HORSERADISH TOPPING:

1 beaten egg	½ C. cider vinegar
3 T. sugar	½ C. water
1 T. (heaping) flour	1 T. butter

Mix all ingredients and cook about 5 minutes, stirring constantly. Cool. When ready to serve whip 1 pkg. Dream Whip and add 1 T. horseradish. Add to above mixture and serve over ham balls.

PORK LOAF RING

1½ lbs. ground smoked picnic shoulder
1¼ lbs. ground fresh pork
1½ C. soft bread crumbs
½ C. chopped onion
2 beaten eggs
½ C. milk

Combine ingredients thoroughly. Press mixture lightly in oiled 6½ cup ring mold; invert in shallow pan. Bake at 350° for 1 hour. Remove from ring mold. Makes 10 servings.

LIVER AND ONIONS

2 lbs. sliced liver
Salt and pepper to taste
2 medium onions
1 can tomato soup

Dip liver slices in flour and quick brown in skillet. Slice one onion on bottom of cooker. Add browned liver and other onion. Spoon on undiluted soup. Cover and set on high 1 hour, turn to low to cook. After 4 hours this can be eaten or will wait up to 10 hours.

HASHED-BROWN OMELET

4 slices bacon
2 C. shredded cooked potatoes (or substitute packaged hash brown potatoes, cooked)
¼ C. chopped onion
¼ C. chopped green pepper
4 eggs
¼ C. milk
1 C. shredded sharp process American cheese

In 10x12-inch skillet, cook bacon until crisp. Leave drippings in skillet; drain bacon and crumble. Mix next 3 ingredients; pat into skillet. Cook over low heat until underside is crisp and brown. Blend eggs, milk, ½ tsp. salt, and dash pepper; pour over potatoes. Top with cheese and bacon. Cover; cook over low heat about 10 minutes. Loosen omelet. Serve in wedges. Serves 4.

Ham-Potato-Cheese Chowder

2 medium potatoes (diced, 2 C.)
1 C. water
1 C. chopped onion
3 T. butter
3½ T. flour

Dash of pepper & salt
3 C. milk
1½ C. small cubed ham
1½ C. (6 oz.) sharp Cheddar cheese

Cook potato in water. Drain, reserving liquid and adding enough water to make 1 cup. Cook onion in butter until tender. Blend in flour, salt, and pepper. Add milk and potato water. Cook until mixture bubbles, stirring constantly. Add ham, potato, and cheese; bring up to heat.

HAM CHOWDER

4 carrots (diced)
4 stalks celery (diced)
1 small onion (diced)
4 potatoes (diced)
5 C. water
2-3 C. diced ham
2 T. butter
Salt & pepper, to taste
6 T. flour
2½ C. milk

Cook carrots, celery, onions and potatoes in 5 C. of water until tender. Add ham, butter, salt and pepper. Blend flour into milk, stir into soup and stir until mixture boils. Turn to very low heat and simmer for 20 minutes. When serving sprinkle top with paprika and chopped parsley.

Sweet and Sour Pork

1½ lbs. lean pork steak (cubed)
½ C. water
1 (20 oz.) can pineapple chunks
1 small green pepper (cut in strips)
2 T. cornstarch
¼ C. vinegar
2½ T. soy sauce
¼ C. chopped onion
Salt to taste
¼ C. brown sugar

Brown pork, add water and simmer 1 hour. Combine brown sugar, juice from pineapple, cornstarch, and vinegar and mix well. Add pineapple chunks, green pepper, onion, soy sauce, and salt. Serve over rice and top with chow mein noodles.

Ham Balls

3 lbs. ground ham
1 lb. ground beef
1 lb. ground pork
3 C. graham crackers (crushed)
2 C. milk
¼ tsp. pepper
3 eggs
1 tsp. salt

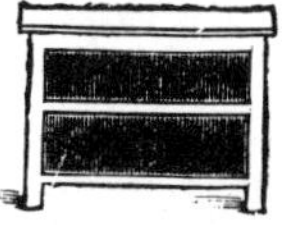

SAUCE:
1 C. water
1 C. brown sugar
1 tsp. mustard
1 C. catsup
¾ C. vinegar

Mix well and shape into balls. Cook in sauce. For Sauce: Boil and pour over ham balls. Bake in 325° oven for 90 minutes. Baste during baking. Serves 32.

Rib-Sticking Good Spareribs

1/2 c. Russian dressing
1-1/2 lb. spareribs, cut into serving
pieces & parboiled
1/4 c. maple syrup

In shallow baking dish, pour dressing over spareribs. Cover & marinate in refigerator, turning occasionally, at least 3 hours. Preheat over to 375 ˚. Remove ribs, reserving marinade. Place ribs in foil-lined baking dish. Bake, turning once & basting frequently with reserved marinade blended with maple syrup, 30 minutes or until ribs are done.

Boston Baked Beans

1 qt. beans
1 small onion
¼ lb. side pork or bacon (cut in pieces)
½-1 T. salt
3-4 T. brown sugar
½ T. mustard
3 T. catsup
3-4 T. molasses (Brer Rabbit)
1 C. hot water

Wash and soak beans in cold water overnight. In the morning drain, cover with fresh water and cook slowly until skins break. Drain. Place onion in bottom of earthenware bean pot. Pour in beans. Add meat. Mix seasonings and hot water together. Add molasses and hot water mixture. Cover bean pot and bake in slow oven for 6-8 hours. Add water from time to time when necessary. Bake uncovered the last hour.

PORK CHOP SUPREME

6-8 pork chops
½ c. water
1 can cream of chicken soup

Dressing:

4 c. bread cubes
1/3 c. chopped celery
¼ c. melted butter
salt & pepper to taste
2 eggs
1 small onion, chopped
2 T. parsley flakes

Brown pork chops and place in roaster. Make dressing by mixing all dressing ingredients together. Spoon dressing onto pork chops. Dilute soup with ½ c. water and pour over chops and dressing. Cover, bake in 350 degree oven for one hour.

Pork Chops and Peas with Mushroom Sauce

6 pork chops
2 pkgs. frozen green peas
½ C. chopped onion
1 can cream of mushroom soup (undiluted)
½ C. milk

Preheat oven to 350°. Trim chops and brown on both sides. Place chops in large, shallow baking dish. Combine peas, onions, soup, and milk in bowl and pour over chops. Cover, bake 1 hour. Uncover and bake another 10 minutes until chops are tender. Serve with buttered noodles.

HAMBALL RECIPE

3 lbs. ground ham
1 lb. hamburger
1 lb. ground pork
3 C. graham crackers (crushed)
3 eggs
2 C. milk
1 tsp. onion salt
1 tsp. salt
1 tsp. liquid smoke
¼ tsp. pepper

SAUCE:
1 can cond. tomato soup
½ can water
1 C. brown sugar
1 T. dry mustard
¼ C. vinegar

Each hamball is to contain ½ C. of meat mixture to make 24. Put sauce over balls before baking. Bake at 325° for 1 hour.

BARBECUED HAM BALLS

1¼ lbs. ground ham
1¼ lbs. hamburger
2 eggs
1 C. crushed graham cracker
1 C. milk

SAUCE:
1 can tomato soup
1¼ C. brown sugar
1 tsp. dry mustard
⅔ C. vinegar

Place meatballs in a large cake pan. Combine the sauce ingredients and pour over meatballs. Serves 10 to 12. Bake at 375° for 1½ hours.

Baked Pork Chops

6 pork chops
1 can cream style corn
1 egg (beaten)
2 T. butter (melted)
2 T. green pepper (opt.)
½ C. cracker crumbs
2 T. chopped onion
1 tsp. sugar

Place browned and seasoned chops in pan or roaster. Mix together the next 7 ingredients and put on top of pork chops. Bake 1 hour in a slow oven, 325°. Serve with baked potatoes and tossed green salad.

Stir-Fried Tenderloin with Vegetables

1 pork loin tenderloin (about ¾ lb.)
3 T. soy sauce
1 T. dry or cooking sherry
2½ tsp. cornstarch
1¼ tsp. sugar
1/8 tsp. ground ginger
Salad oil
½ bunch broccoli (cut into bite-size pieces)
½ lb. mushrooms (sliced)
1 carrot (thinly sliced)
¼ tsp. salt
2 T. water

About 30 minutes before serving, slice loin crosswise into 1/8-inch slices. In bowl mix pork with next 5 ingredients. In skillet over high heat in 3 T. hot oil, cook broccoli, mushrooms, carrots, and salt, stirring quickly and frequently until vegetables are coated with oil. Add water and stir-fry until vegetables are tender-crisp. Spoon vegetables onto warm platter; keep warm. In same skillet over high heat in 2 T. hot oil, cook pork mixture until pork loses its pink color, about 2-3 minutes, stirring quickly and frequently. Return vegetables to skillet and stir-fry until heated through. Makes 3 servings.

BARBECUED WIENERS

6 slices chopped bacon
3 large onions (diced)
1 T. vinegar
1 T. sugar
1 tsp. Worcestershire sauce
1 pinch of clove powder
1 (10½ oz.) can tomato soup
1½ dozen wieners

Fry bacon and onions until brown. Add remaining ingredients; except wieners, simmer for a few minutes and then pour over wieners that have been placed in shallow baking pan. Bake at 325° for 45 minutes.

SQUARE DANCE REUBAN

2 lbs. ground pork
¾ c. chopped sauerkraut
½ t. caraway seed

6 slices Swiss cheese (3"x2")
salt
6 sesame seed round buns
(split and toasted)

Heat sauerkraut and caraway seed; keep warm. Divide ground pork into 6 equal portions and shape into patties ½ inch thick. Place patties on rack in broiler pan so top of meat is 3 inches from heat. Broil 6 minutes, sprinkle with salt, turn and broil second side 4 minutes. Place piece of cheese on each patty and broil until cheese melts and patties are done. Drain warm sauerkraut thoroughly and place on bottom half of bun. Place patties on sauerkraut. Place top half of bun on sandwich and enjoy. Makes 6 sandwiches.

Broccoli, Ham & Pasta Casserole

1/2 can broccoli cheese soup
1/2 c. milk
1-1/2 tsp spicy brown mustard or Dijon-style mustard
1 c. broccoli (fresh or frozen)
1-1/2 c. cooked shell macaroni (1 c. dry)
4 oz. (3/4 c.) cooked ham, cut in thin strips

In skillet, combine soup, milk & mustard. Add broccoli & heat to boiling over medium heat. Reduce heat to low. Cover & cook 5 minutes or until broccoli is tender. Add macaroni & ham & heat thoroughly.

PORK CHOP CASSEROLE

6 large pork chops	1 large onion
milk & salt & pepper	1 med. head cabbage

Brown chops in a little butter or oleo. Turn and brown other side and slice on the onion. Put in large casserole. Shred cabbage fine and press over chops and onions. Pour enough milk over chops to barely cover. Add seasonings to taste. Bake covered for 55 to 60 minutes at 350 degrees. We always serve this with baked potatoes, dipping some of the milk that's left in the bottom over them.

CHEESE HAM CASSEROLE

2 c. cut up ham
2 c. milk
1 can cream of celery soup
¼ c. onions (chopped)
½ t. salt
2 c. uncooked noodles (broken up slightly)
1 can cream of mushroom soup
2 c. Cracker Barrel cheese (grated)
1 can mushrooms (optional)

Mix ingredients and place in greased 9x13 in. pan. Cover and refrigerate overnight. Bake for about 45 minutes at 350 degrees until bubbly. You might want to try chicken in place of ham.

Pork Chops & Vegetables

2 boneless pork chops, 3/4" thick
1 Tbsp margarine
2 oz. mushrooms
1/2 can cream of mushroom soup
4-1/2 oz. frozen green beans
1 Tbsp water

In skillet over medium-high heat, cook chops in margarine for 10 minutes or until browned on both sides. Add remaining ingredients & heat to boiling. Reduce heat to low, cover & cook 10 minutes or until chops are no longer pink & beans are tender. Serve over hot cooked egg noodles.

Pork Chops

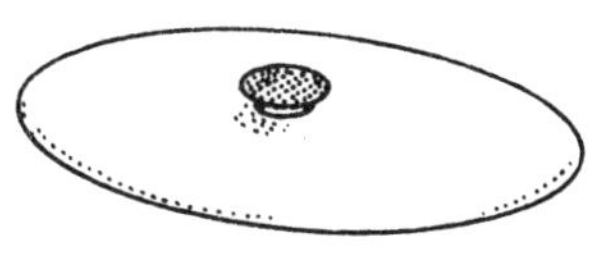

2 pork chops
mustard (jar, not dry)
salt & pepper, to taste
brown sugar
crushed corn flakes
milk

Spread mustard on chops. Salt & pepper them. Place in casserole. Drip a bit of brown sugar over each. Sprinkle crushed corn flakes on top. Pour milk around the chops to almost cover. Bake at 350° for 1-1/2 hours.

Broccoli, Ham & Cheese Casserole

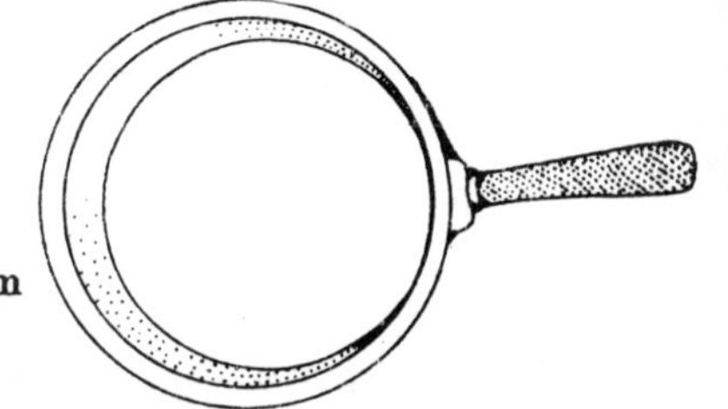

1/2 head fresh or frozen broccoli
1/2 small jar Cheez Whiz
2 Tbsp milk
1 thick slice ham
bread crumbs

Cook broccoli 5 minutes in boiling water. In a small pan melt cheese & milk. Put broccoli in a baking dish. Put chunks of ham on top of broccoli. Pour cheese sauce on top. Sprinkle bread crumbs over top. Cook at 350° until bread crumbs are brown.

Eggs Brunch

4 slices bacon (sliced)
½ lb. chipped beef (coarsley sliced)
¼ C. butter
1 lb. fresh mushrooms (sliced and sauteed)
½ C. flour
1 qt. whole milk
16 eggs
1 C. evaporated milk
¼ tsp. salt
¼ C. melted butter
Pepper

Saute bacon and drain; remove from pan. In the same pan add chipped beef, butter, and ¾ of the mushrooms. Sprinkle flour and pepper over mixture. Gradually stir in whole milk. Heat mixture, stirring until thick and smooth. Set aside. Combine eggs with salt and evaporated milk and scramble in butter. In a 3-qt. casserole dish, alternate layers of eggs and sauce, ending with sauce. Garnish with reserved mushrooms. Refrigerate overnight. Before serving, cover and bake 1-1½ hours at 275°.

PORK STEAKS

4 pork shoulder steaks (½'' thick)
1 T. lard or drippings
1 tsp. salt
1/8 tsp. pepper
1 (1 lb. 13 oz.) can sauerkraut (drained)
1 (16 oz.) can tomatoes (drained)
1 tsp. instant minced onion

Brown pork steaks in drippings. Pour off drippings. Season with salt and pepper. Combine sauerkraut, tomatoes, and onion. Pour on top of sauerkraut mixture. Cover tightly and bake in a moderate oven for 30 minutes. Remove cover and continue baking for 30 minutes or until meat is done. Makes 4 servings.

CAULIFLOWER-HAM BAKE

1 large head cauliflower
2 T. butter or margarine
3 T. all-purpose flour
1½ C. milk

1½ C. shredded sharp American cheese (6 oz.)
2 C. cubed, fully cooked ham
¼ C. fine dry bread crumbs
1 T. butter or margarine (melted)

Break cauliflower into flowerets (should have about 5 C.); cook in boiling salted water until tender, about 10 minutes. Drain thoroughly; set aside. In saucepan, melt the 2 T. butter or margarine. Stir in flour, add milk all at once. Cook and stir until thickened and bubbly. Add cheese and stir until melted. Stir in cooked cauliflower and ham. Turn into a 2-qt. casserole. Combine crumbs and the melted butter; sprinkle over top. Bake uncovered at 350° until heated through, 30-35 minutes. Makes 6 servings. Excellent for school athletic banquets.

Pork Chops 'N Stuffing

4 pork chops
3 C. soft bread crumbs
2 T. chopped onions
¼ C. melted butter
¼ C. water
¼ tsp. poultry seasoning
1 can mushroom soup
⅓ C. water

Brown chops and place in baking dish. Lightly mix together bread crumbs, butter, ¼ C. water, onion and poultry seasoning. Place a mound of stuffing on each chop. Blend soup with ⅓ C. water and pour over chops. Bake at 350° for 1 hour.

Glazed Pork Chops

6 lean pork chops
6 onion slices
½ tsp. salt
Dash of pepper
1 chicken bouillon cube or
1 tsp. instant
2 tsp. prepared mustard
¼ C. water

Brown chops in frying pan. Place onion slices in a single layer in a shallow baking dish; top each with a browned chop and season. Combine bouillon cube, mustard, and water in a cup. Drizzle mixture over chops and cover. Bake at 350° for 45 minutes or until chops are tender.

BARBECUED SPARE RIBS

4 lb. spare ribs
1 C. diced onion
1 C. catsup or chili sauce
1 C. water
2 tsp. salt
2 tsp. Worcestershire sauce
½ C. vinegar
¼ C. brown sugar
2 tsp. dry mustard
½ tsp. chili powder

Mix all of the ingredients and pour over spare ribs. Bake in oven for 1¾ hours at 350°. Bake uncovered the last 15 minutes.

SWEET AND SOUR PORK CHOPS

12 med. pork chops, cut ½ inch thick
½ c. pure vegetable oil
2 green peppers, cut in squares
4 T. cornstarch
2 t. salt
½ c. vinegar
2 c. sliced celery
2 small onions, cut in ⅛'s
½ c. brown sugar
1 c. orange juice
1 - 27½ oz. can Hunt's Manwich
1 - 20 oz. can sliced pineapple undrained and quartered.

Trim fat from pork chops. Brown in oil in large skillet. Remove and set aside. Add to skillet: green peppers, celery and onion. Saute slightly. Drain fat and mix cornstarch and brown sugar, add to skillet with remaining ingredients. Cook, stirring constantly until thickened. Return chops to skillet, cover and simmer 30-40 minutes over low heat. Stir once or twice. (I suggest you use a very large electric skillet.)

SWEET & SOUR SPARERIBS

3 lbs. spareribs or pork shoulder steak, cut into 1½-inch pieces
2 T. cornstarch
1 clove garlic, minced fine
1 slice ginger root, minced
½ c. water
2 to 3 T. salad oil
1 T. brown sugar
2 T. soy sauce
¾ c. white vinegar
4 to 5 T. brown sugar

Combine pork, corn starch, 1 T. brown sugar and soy sauce. Let stand 15 minutes or more. Saute garlic and ginger root in salad oil; add pork and brown on all sides. Add vinegar, brown sugar and water (taste to adjust sweetness). When mixture comes to a boil, turn to low heat and simmer 45 minutes to one hour or until pork is tender (do not overcook). Serve with steamed rice. Note: To thicken gravy, add cornstarch and water.

MEAT POT PIE

I was taught to use ham or chicken. Cook until soft, then take meat from broth and cut up fine. Cut potatoes in cubes and cook along with meat. Some people just use potatoes instead of meat. Then add butter. Make dough of sweet cream, work in flour until real stiff. Roll out and cut in squares. Cook for 15 minutes or more. If broth is not salty add salt to dough.

POT PIE

8 T. flour
1½ t. baking powder
a little salt
2 eggs
sweet milk to make a dough

Cook from 10 to 15 minutes.

BAR-B-Q HAM

12 lbs. chopped ham
10 T. vinegar
10 small onions (chopped)
5 c. catsup
2 c. brown sugar

Mix catsup, sugar, vinegar and onions. Pour on chipped ham. Bake one hour in oven until hot. Could be heated on top of stove also. Serve on buns.

EASTER HAM

1 lb. ground ham
½ lb. ground pork
1½ lb. ground beef
salt & pepper
2 eggs (beaten)
1 c. cracker crumbs
1 c. milk

Mix the above ingredients together. Shape into loaf and place in baking dish or roasting pan. Make a glaze out of 1 c. brown sugar, 1 t. mustard, 1/3 c. vinegar, ½ c. water. Mix all together and cook about 5 minutes. Pour over the ham loaf and bake for 1½ hours covered with ½ hour uncovered at 350 degrees.

Orange Honey Glazed Ham

1 (3 lb.) canned ham
1 (3 oz.) pkg. orange gelatin
2 T. onion, chopped
1 tsp. ground cloves
1 T. honey

Drain ham; rub surface with cloves. Place ham on a large sheet of heavy-duty aluminum foil. Place on rack in baking pan. Sprinkle dry gelatin over ham and drizzle with honey. Close foil with "grocery store" fold. Bake at 350° for 1 hour. Open foil, being careful to avoid steam, and bake another 30 minutes. Serves 8 to 10.

Green Beans and Sausage

1 lb. green beans
2 T. chopped onion
1 (12 oz.) pkg. link sausages

Clean and snap beans. Place in kettle and cover with water. Add onion and cut-up sausages. Cover and simmer until beans are barely tender. Serves 3 to 4.

SOUP AND SAUSAGE CASSEROLE

(Quite a change for a crowd-conscious casserole - a colorful and tasty rice mixture paired with delicately browned pork sausage patties.)

6 lbs. pork sausage
4 C. chopped celery
4 medium onions (chopped, about 2 C.)
2 C. chopped green pepper
4 C. uncooked regular rice
6 (2 oz. ea.) envelopes dry chicken noodle soup mix
⅔ C. toasted slivered almonds
½ tsp. saffron*
3 qts. boiling water
Snipped parsley

Heat oven to 350°. Shape sausage into 48 patties or, if sausage is in rolls, cut each roll into 8 slices. Brown sausage in large skillet over medium-low heat about 3-4 minutes on each side; remove and drain. Pour fat from skillet, leaving just enough to coat bottom. Add celery, onion, and green pepper; cook and stir until onion is tender. In each of 4 ungreased baking pans, 13x9x2-inches, mix ¼ of the onion mixture (about 1½ C.), 1 C. rice, 1½ envelopes soup mix and ¼ of the almonds. Dissolve saffron in boiling water; stir 3 C. into each pan. Arrange 12 sausage patties on mixture in each pan. Cover; bake about 45 minutes or until rice is tender and liquid is absorbed. Garnish with snipped parsley. (Makes 24 servings, 2 sausage patties and 4½-inch square rice mixture per serving.) *If desired, omit saffron; add 10 drops yellow food color to each pan with the boiling water.

Maple Baked Beans

1 lb. dry navy beans
4 qt. water, divided
6 slices bacon, cut, or
  1 c. cooked ham cubes
1 med. onion, chopped
1 c. maple syrup
1/2 c. catsup
1/4 c. barbecue sauce
5 tsp. cider vinegar
1 tsp. salt
1/2 tsp. pepper

Soft and rinse beans, place in 4-quart Dutch oven. Cover with 2 quarts cold water. Bring to a boil; reduce heat and simmer 2 minutes. Remove from heat. Cover and let stand 1 hour. Drain and rinse beans. Return beans to Dutch oven, cover with remaining water. Bring to boil, reduce heat and simmer 30 to 40 minutes, or until almost tender. Drain and reserve liquid. In a 2 1/2-quart casserole, combine beans with all remaining ingredients. Bake, covered, at 300° for 2 1/2 hours, or until tender (cooking times may vary considerably). Stir occasionally, add reserved liquid if necessary. Yields 10 to 12 generous portions.

When I prepare these beans, they often require considerably more cooking time. The recipe can also be easily prepared in crock-pot. Once beans are cooked, place all ingredients in the crock-pot. Stir gently to mix. Cook on low for 10 to 12 hours.

BACON AND EGG BAKE

6 slices bacon
2 med. onions, sliced
1 can cream of mushroom soup
¼ c. milk
5 hard cooked eggs, sliced
2 c. shredded cheese (optional)
dash of salt & pepper
English muffins - split & toasted

Heat oven to 350 degrees. Fry bacon until crisp, remove from skillet. Drain fat, reserving 2 T. and saute onions in bacon fat. Stir in soup, milk, cheese and seasonings. Pour into 10"x6" baking dish; top with crumbled bacon. Bake 20 minutes. Serve over split, toasted muffins or toasted bread. Serves 6 to 8.

SAUCEY PORK CHOPS (Easy and Delicious)

Pork chops
1 can cream of mushroom soup
Little milk
½ can sour cream
½ can fried onion rings

Brown pork chops. Mix and pour over meat the cream of mushroom soup, milk, sour cream, and onion rings. Bake at 350° for 1 hour. Last 5 minutes, add remaining onion rings.

Butter Beans

2⅔ C. dried butter beans or lima beans
3 qts. water
½ C. chopped onion
1 tsp. salt
6 strips bacon or ham hocks

Soak beans in water overnight. Or, bring to a boil, simmer 3 minutes, and let stand for 1 hour. Rinse, cover with water; add onion and bacon (or ham hocks). Simmer, uncovered for about 30 to 40 minutes until beans are tender. Add salt and simmer another 4 to 5 minutes.

HAM BALLS

2 lbs. ham loaf
1 lb. ground beef
3 eggs
3 C. graham cracker crumbs
2 C. milk
Salt & pepper

Mix all together and make into balls.

SAUCE:
2 cans tomato soup
1½ C. brown sugar
½ C. vinegar
2 T. mustard

Pour sauce over balls and bake at 350° for 1 hour.

CORN AND PORK

4 to 6½-inch pork chops
1 T. prepared mustard
1 (1 lb.) can (2 C.) golden cream corn
⅔ C. soft bread (cubed)
2 T. onion (chopped)
1 T. green pepper (chopped)
1 tsp. salt
Dash of pepper
½ C. water

Spread pork chops with mustard. Dip in eggs and roll in cracker crumbs; brown well. Combine corn, bread crumbs, onion, green pepper, salt, and pepper. Arrange chops in 1-layer in baking dish. Drain grease from pan and stir in ½ C. water and bring to a boil. Pour over chops. Top with corn mixture, cover and bake at 350° for 15 minutes. Uncover and bake for 45 minutes more.

Spuds

1 dozen VERY small new potatoes
¼ C. sour cream or yogurt
1 T. grated carrot
1 T. chopped green onion & tops
4 slices bacon,
crisp & crumbled

Boil the potatoes until tender. When cool, peel and slice into halves. Using a teaspoon, hollow out centers. Stir together sour cream, carrot, and onion. Fill potatoes with this mixture and top with crumbled bacon. Serves 3 to 4.

Goodie Casserole

4 pork chops
4 medium potatoes (sliced)
1 can cream of mushroom soup
2 medium onions (sliced)
Velveeta cheese

Place chops in pan; salt and pepper. Cover with potato slices; then sliced onions, a layer of cheese; spread with a can of soup and another layer of cheese. Cover and bake at 350° for 1 hour.

BEAN CASSEROLE

⅓ lb. bacon
½ lb. hamburger
1 (No. 2½) can pork and beans
1 (No. 303) can green beans
1 (No. 303) can lima beans
½ C. brown sugar
¼ C. white sugar
⅓ C. catsup
1 medium onion

Chop onion and brown in skillet with hamburger and chopped bacon. Mix the rest of ingredients in casserole. Add browned meats. Bake 1 hour at 350°. This is a good recipe to use if you're feeding a crowd. You can add more pork and beans and it really doesn't take away from it.

GRAVY BAKED PORK CHOPS

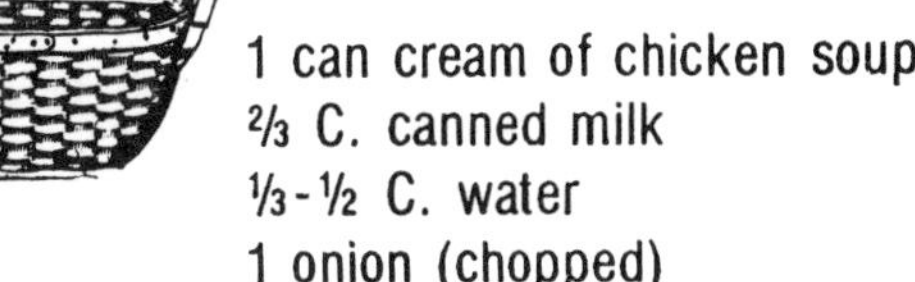

¼ tsp. salt
Dash of pepper
4-6 lean pork chops
1 T. shortening

1 can cream of chicken soup
⅔ C. canned milk
⅓-½ C. water
1 onion (chopped)

Sprinkle salt and pepper over chops. Melt shortening in pan. Brown chops on both sides; drain off fat. Mix soup milk, water, and onion. Pour over chops and bake at 350° for 45 minutes or until chops are tender. Stir gravy well. Serve with mashed potatoes.

DAY'S END

1 lb. hamburger
1 lb. ground pork
½ C. chopped onion
1 T. Worcestershire sauce
3 eggs
1½ C. cracker crumbs (fine)
1 (8 oz.) can tomato sauce
Salt
Pepper

Mix and shape into balls or loaves, whichever preferred. Place in pan, bake, covered at 350° for 45 minutes. Uncover, pour off grease, pour ketchup and brown sugar sauce over top, bake for 20 more minutes.

BARBECUED COUNTRY RIBS

3 lbs. ribs (cut into portions)
½ C. pineapple juice
½ C. dark corn syrup
2 T. soy sauce
1 tsp. salt

Mix sauce ingredients and pour over ribs in shallow pan. Marinate for 1 to 2 hours. Heat oven to 350°. Roast ribs in pan for 1½ hours or until tender. Turn several times and brush with marinade during roasting.

PORK CHOP CASSEROLE

4 pork chops	1 can cream-style corn

Brown chops and put in casserole; cover with the cream-style corn. Bake at 350° for about 50 minutes or until tender. This is so easy, but so tasty.

PORK CHOPS POTATO BAKE

5 or 6 pork chops
Raw, sliced potatoes
Salt & pepper
Minced onion
1 can cream of mushroom soup
1 can Cheddar cheese soup

Brown pork chops. Slice enough potatoes to half fill a 9x13-inch buttered pan. Sprinkle with salt, pepper, and onion, to taste. Combine soups and pour half over potatoes. Lay pork chops over potatoes and cover with remaining soup. Bake, covered at 350° for 1 hour or until potatoes are done. Uncover and bake until brown.

Deviled Snorter

2 lbs. tenderized ¾-inch pork steak
4 T. oil
1 C. tomato sauce
2 large chopped onions
3 T. vinegar
1 T. mustard
4 tsp. horseradish
2 cloves minced garlic
1 tsp. salt
1 tsp. pepper
1½ C. water
2 T. soy sauce

Trim excess fat from meat, cut meat into serving sizes. Dredze meat in flour. Brown in hot oil. Place in deep dish ovenproof glass or roaster. Layer onions on top of meat. Mix together the tomato sauce, vinegar, mustard, horseradish, garlic, salt, pepper, water, and soy sauce. Pour over meat. Bake 1 hour at 350° uncovered. Serve with hot buttered noodles or hot rice.

Favorite Egg-Sausage Casserole

1½ lbs. ground sausage
9 eggs
½ tsp. dry mustard
1½ C. grated cheddar cheese
3 slices bread (cubed)
3 C. whole milk

Brown sausage; drain. Beat eggs slightly. Combine rest of ingredients. Place in ungreased 9×13-inch pan. Refrigerate overnight. Take out 1 hour before baking. Bake at 350° for 45 minutes. (If not put out ahead of time, bake at 300° for 1½ hours.)

Meatball Soup (Kafta)

1 small onion
Salt & pepper, to taste
½ lb. ground beef
½ C. parsley (chopped fine)
Butter or margarine

6-8 C. cold water
1 cinnamon stick
½ C. uncooked rice
1 ripe tomato (diced) (optional)

Finely mince onion and mix with salt and pepper, to taste. Add meat and few leaves of parsley; mix well. Make meatballs the size of walnuts. Brown the meatballs in butter. Add small amount of water to skillet to remove residue. Empty meatballs and stock into saucepan and add cinnamon stick and remaining water. Let boil on medium for 10 minutes, then add rice and tomato, and additional salt, to taste. Cook for about 30 minutes or until rice is tender. Add remaining parsley during the last 5 minutes.

CHURCH CASSEROLE

2 T. butter
¼ C. flour
1¼ C. milk
¼ tsp. salt
½ lb. cubed cheddar cheese

1 qt. chopped cooked potatoes
1 lb. ham (cubed)
10 oz. pkg. frozen mixed vegetables (cooked)

Make white sauce of butter, flour, milk, salt and pepper. Add cheese. Stir until melted. Put other ingredients in casserole and pour cheese sauce over them. Bake at 325° for 45 minutes. Adjust temperature for your oven.

SWEET AND SOUR MEATBALLS

1 lb. lean ground beef
1 tsp. salt
½ tsp. pepper
½ green pepper (finely chopped)
1 C. soft bread crumbs
(soaked in ½ C. milk)

SAUCE:
½ C. onion (chopped)
6 T. sugar
½ C. water
½ C. catsup
2 T. Worcestershire sauce
2 T. vinegar

Combine the first 5 ingredients and form into walnut-sized ball. Put in a casserole and add the sauce. Bake, covered at 350° for 1 hour. Serve over rice.

MISCELLANEOUS

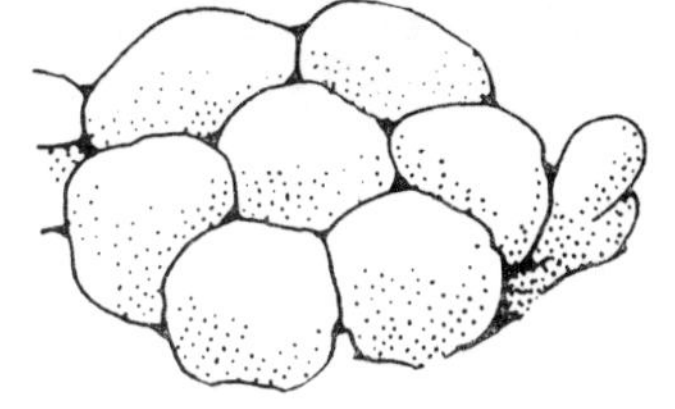

Misc.

HOMEMADE SALAMI

1 lb. hamburger
1 lb. ground pork
¼ tsp. salt
¼ tsp. pepper
1/8 tsp. garlic powder
1 T. liquid smoke
1 T. mustard seed or powder
2 T. Morton Tender Quick
¾ C. water

Mix well. Divide mixture evenly. Place on foil and make a roll. Wrap and refrigerate 24 hours. Unwrap, place on rack and bake 1 hour at 350°. Cool and serve.

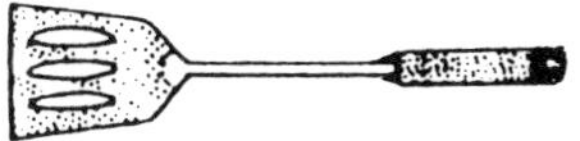

HAND-ROLLED GARLIC SAUSAGE

1 lb. ground veal
2 lbs. ground pork
1 lb. pork sausage
8 cloves garlic (minced)
1 T. rubbed sage
1 tsp. marjoram
Salt and pepper

Makes 3 dozen. Combine ground meats and regrind. Add spices and garlic and grind again. Roll the meat into 1 oz. balls (about the size of a golf ball) and then into cigar shapes about 3-inches long. At this point the sausages can be frozen. Fry the sausages in a skillet over medium-high heat.

CHEESE BALL

¾ C. finely chopped ham
8 oz. pkg. cream cheese (softened)
1 C. grated Velveeta cheese
1 tsp. minced onion
1 tsp. Worcestershire sauce
¼ - ½ C. finely chopped ham (to roll in)

Mix all ingredients well. Roll cheese ball in finely chopped ham.

Nachos

1/2 lb. ground beef
1/2 lb. pork sausage
1 lg. onion
2 (16 oz.) cans refried beans
1 (4 oz.) can chopped, mild, green chilies
3 c. (12 oz.) grated Monterey Jack cheese
3/4 c. taco sauce (bottled)
1/4 c. green onion
1 avocado, mashed
1 c. sour cream

Remove the sausage from the casing; crumble in skillet. Sauté sausage, beef and onion until brown. Drain grease and add salt to taste. In baking dish (10x15-inch), spread beans on bottom; top evenly with meat mixture. Cover with chilies; drizzle taco sauce over top. Bake, uncovered, for 20 to 25 minutes at 400°. About half-way through, add cheese. Remove; sprinkle with onions. Put mound of avocado in center and dollops of sour cream all over. Serve with tortilla chips.

ANYDAY DRESSING

1 onion (chopped fine)
4 T. bacon drippings
8-10 slices bread (cubed)
(4-5 C. dry bread)

1 tsp. sage
½ C. celery (chopped)
1 C. chicken broth
or 1 can chicken and rice soup
with ½ can water

Brown the onion in the bacon drippings. Add to rest of ingredients and mix well. Pour into well greased baking dish. Cover and bake at 325° for about 1 hour or bake in a greased ring mold.

MINI COOKBOOKS

(Only 3-1/2x5) with Maxi Good Eatin' - 160 to 192 pages - $5.95

*MINNESOTA COOKING
*WISCONSIN COOKIN'
*SUPER SIMPLE COOKING
*APHRODISIAC COOKING
*GOOD COOKIN' FROM
THE PLAIN PEOPLE
*COOKIN WITH THINGS
THAT GO SPLASH
*OHIO COOKIN'
*APPLES! APPLIES! APPLIES!
*CITRUS! CITRUS! CITRUS!

*IOWA COOKING
*DAKOTA COOKIN'
*PREGNANT LADY COOKING
*MIDWEST SMALL TOWN
*INDIANA COOKIN'
*KANSAS COOKIN'
*BERRIES! BERRIES!
*PEACHES! PEACHES!
*MISSOURI COOKIN'
*MICHIGAN COOKIN'
*OFF TO COLLEGE COOKBOOK

*OREGON COOKING
*KID PUMPKIN FUN BOOK
*NEW JERSEY GOOKING
*PENNSYLVANIA COOKING
*NUTS! NUTS! NUTS!
*COOKIN' WITH THINGS THAT
GO CLUCK
*WORKING GIRL COOKING
*PUMPKINS! PUMPKINS
*NEW YORK COOKING
*KID COOKIN'

*ILLINOIS COOKIN"
*ARKANSAS COOKIN'
*IDAHO COOKING
*WASHINGTON COOKIN'
*COOKING WITH SPIRITS
*CHERRIES! CHERRIES!
*HILL COUNTRY COOKIN'
* COOKING WITH THINGS GO OINK
*POTATOES! POTATOES!
*COOKING WITH THINGS THAT GO MOO
*THE KID'S GARDEN FUN BOOK

IN BETWEENIE COOKBOOKS

(5-1/2x8-1/2) - 150 pages - $9.95

* HUNTING IN THE NUDE COOKBOOK
*II-KON-GEE INIZAN MAAZINA 'IGANS (Ojibwa for "to-have-a-feast cooking recipes")
*HERBAL COOKERY
*MOTORCYCLER'S WILD CRITTER COOKBOOK
*SOCCOR MOM COOKBOOK
* INDIAN COOKING COOKBOOK
*COOKING a la NUDE
*THE COW PUNCHER'S COOKBOOK
*THE ADAPTABLE APPLE
*MAD ABOUT GARLIC
*TURN-OF-THE-CENTURY COOKBOOK